Journey of Intertwined Souls

Nguyet Luna Truong

BookLeaf
Publishing

India | USA | UK

Presentation by *BookLeaf Publishing*

Web: www.bookleafpub.com

E-mail: info@bookleafpub.com

ISBN: 9789363307575

First edition 2024

ACKNOWLEDGEMENT

I am deeply grateful to everyone who has supported and inspired me on this poetic journey.

To the muse whose presence and influence have shaped these poems, thank you for the spiritual connection that sparked my writing.

To my family and friends, whose encouragement and understanding have sustained me throughout this creative process.

To the anonymous readers and supporters, thank you for your openness and willingness to explore the interwoven tapestry of life through poetry.

Warm regards,

Nguyet Luna Truong

PREFACE

Welcome to "Journey of Intertwined Souls". This collection explores the profound connection between two souls—how lives intersect, influence each other, and evolve through love, spirituality, and shared experiences.

Through these poems, I delve into moments of intimacy, longing, and the transformative power of the relationship. Each verse reflects an exploration of this spiritual journey and the enduring bond that shapes life's tapestry.

I invite you to embark on this poetic journey with me, where souls intertwine across time and space, navigating the complexities of fate and choice. May these poems resonate with you, offering moments of reflection and inspiration as we explore the interconnected tapestry of existence.

Warm regards,

Nguyet Luna Truong

Dreams in Reality

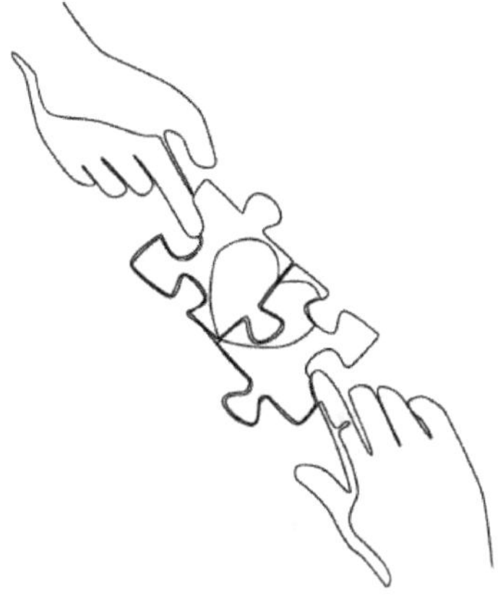

No days pass without my longing, you'll never
truly know
On this spiral I'm spinning, love me as I grow

You come into my life, cool summer breeze in
winter's grip,
Quick warm hug, your shining smile in cold
February's slip.
I'll never imagine how our love story began like
this,
Warm melting cold heart to my ultimate bliss.

Will you ever know my endless love's pure
clarity,
Or is it always just a dream in reality?

You opened up to me, as I did to you,
Things happened so naturally, as if on cue.
You were so kind with your smile, gentle and
true,
You were so soft, you made me weak, in
everything you do.
I could not let go of you, my heart's anchor, my
love so true.

We know we've connected before, I see the Déjà
vu,
When I saw you standing, waiting there, it all
felt true.
I knew I had known you before, before we even
met,
At the crowded station, I didn't need to fret.
I recognized you right away, as if we'd met
before,
Our souls intertwined, fate knocking at the door.

Replaying this time all over in my head,
I know we've met somewhere, words left unsaid.
I truly do remember, you're so familiar to me,
Completely comfortable, with you so free.

Being around you feels so right,
My dear sweetheart, a spell in sight?
Or did I forget to drink *Wang Qing Shui,
Forget love potion, in haste to be with you.

In this life, I remember everything,
From our previous life, fate's whispering.
I recall it now, our intertwined fate,
You've turned dreams into my reality's gate.

* "Wang Qing Shui" is the potion that everyone
must drink before reincarnation to forget
everything that happened in their previous life.

Echoes Across Realms

Your smile fades as your shadow looms,
Reflect in your eyes, I see it bloom.
What magic is it that I possess?
You know it's in you, no need to guess.

"We said let's stay in the moment," I agreed with you,
"You said tomorrow will be our reality," I questioned, naive.
You always smile, hiding something deep within,
A mystery in your eyes, a secret you keep unseen.

"What kind of reality awaits us," I wonder aloud,
In the shadow of our whispers, where truth are allowed.
Your smile, a veil, betrays a hidden truth,
Yet in its warmth, I find solace and youth.

In this moment, the strike of telepathy,
You and I come together, drenched in wine.
I thought this night could be the end,
Just you and me, eternally intertwined.

Our connection, just begun, so naive,
Innocent, we believed it would fade.
Yet, it's just a genesis of our telepathy,
A journey unfolding in shadows, you and me.

Misunderstood Strength

Easy to cry, not a sign of weakness in me,
Silent cares, yet my heart deeply does care.
Brief moment matter, they're not meaningless,
Honest soul, amidst your suspicious bare.

In your eyes, depths of thought I see,
A thinker, tangled in scenarios deep.
Your mind spins, every night, untold,
Spiraling through thoughts, yet to unfold.

Reflecting on my thoughts and feelings,
Knowing myself deeply, revealing.
I earnestly share with you my heart,
Hoping for acceptance, never apart.

Once upon a time, an unexpected love may find,
Will your logical mind embrace it in kind?
A wave of emotions floods through every vein,
Beyond mere infatuation, a bond to sustain.

How we catch feelings may differ,
I plead for your understanding.
Let suspicion be not punished, but celebrated,
Forever seeking each other, two hearts as one.

Psychic Symphony

The distance parts us, how many moons,
I am me, you are you, in silent tunes.
Back to our daily routine, life's refrain,
I bet this is the reality you once explained.

This reality we face is brutal, more than I
thought,
The thought of you repeats, a relentless knot.
Only works and goals can save me now,
From entering this void that distance does allow.

But the gap between us is merely physical miles,
Halfway across the world, our separation
compiles.
Yet why does my heart echo this same steady
beat,
Our cardiovascular rhythms mirror, a symphony
sweet.

I don't chase signs of coincidence,
They manifest daily in my existence.
Across the world, do you witness these scenes?
Beautiful manifestations of our connection's
serene.

You and I mirror the same ways as twin,
Yet we're stubborn to admit this truth within.
My higher divine lifts me, wings spread wide,
I await the day you'll stand by my side.

Like An Old Friend

The old trauma kicks in,
Confidence fades, where to begin?
Your truth shatters me, breaks my guard,
I never knew this pain could hit so hard.

I should have stayed still and quiet,
Held my thoughts, kept them from sight.
You listened attentively, without a glare,
Like an old friend, always there to care.

Let's be honest this night,
Uncomfortably clear, no need to fight.
No sugar-coating, our truths laid bare,
Yet you keep harmony, with tender care.

Lost in your thoughts, it seems,
You said you're okay, in quiet dream.
There's much more than meet the eye,
Your gaze fixed on the ceiling 'til dawn, asking
why.

I trusted you completely,
No reason why, just our soul's decree.
You pour my heart out, this cup brims,
Yet my arms find yours, where sleep begins.
Forgetting an old friend, a grievous wrong,
You woke me, asking if it was a nightmare all
along.
All I wanted to say, with you close by my side,
Is how happy I am, with you as my guide.
Is this a dream? Are you really here with me,
Or is it the sweetest reality, I longed to see?

The Daring Heart

Two hearts, distinct in their essence,
I knew from the start, a cautious presence.
Telling myself to maintain my distance,
A reminder to cherish, to make it last.

Why my gut warned, I couldn't ignore,
Entering love's game, seeking something more.
My honesty stands, unwavering and clear,
Hoping you'll see this golden heart, sincere.

I knew you wanted it light and free,
Like air on your chart, floating serenely.
I hesitate to halt this affection's flow,
For I've found myself falling deeper, I know.

I've hidden these feelings deep inside,
Fearful they might unsettle and divide.
Yearning for our talks, your sweet embrace.
Love's bruising touch, leaving a tender trace.

Do you dream of me in the night,
In my dreams, your absence in sight.
This pause we're in, a temporary state,
Awaiting the moment we resume, fate.

On my end, it continues to grow,
Love, unconditional, starts to show.
Maybe you're unaware, yet here it stands,
A wall rising between, love in my hands.

Invisible Grip

While I feel closer, your intention fades,
Unexpected emotions in fate's cascade.
No plans for this heart's sway,
Just the rhythm of destiny at play.

Your harmony, it captivates,
Leaving me breathless, as it resonates.
You crave the balance, in every scene,
Your control, a silent, guiding stream.

It messes with my mind, a subtle game,
Your unseen grip, a quiet flame.
Each day, new ways you find,
Silently hurting, leaving scars undefined.

Indirectly affecting those in sight,
Since then, a heaviness I can't fight.
Your insecurities seem to play a part,
Don't worry, I'd kiss them away from your heart.

I'll take my leave for a while,
Realizing belatedly, my mistake in style.
Seems like what you're seeking,
With life's burdens heavy, speaking.

Patience guides me, steady and true,
Waiting around your eyes' soft hue.
In this parallel world, a dream we embrace,
Our frequencies entwined, in time and space.

Matching Jackets

It's finally here, the other half,
One for you there, one for me here.
After all the waiting and the wondering,
Now we can breathe easily, without fear.

So warm, like your embrace,
This matching jacket, it's you.
Apart, yet their souls intertwine ,
In a shade, "green yet not quite green."

You bury its half to switch to summer,
I unearth its half to summon summer.
Your coping mechanism, it seems,
Is burying feelings deep within.

Your posts tally up like hidden feelings,
Thankfully, no need to decode those.
In my dreams, your telepathy whispers,
Telling me you must journey elsewhere.

You hide from your feelings, a tactic to stay
strong,
Focusing on positivity, all along.
Your father's wisdom, I deeply respect,
Yet my emotions, my truth, I won't neglect.
In fleeting moments of lovey dovey's sweet
delight,
They fulfill instant needs, yet fade from sight.
I yearn with patience, pondering why I insist,
This unexpected gift, love's essence I persist.

Crossroads of Reflection

Our paths to reclaim ourselves anew,
Each step strengthens, each moment true.
Youthful hearts, troubled deep within,
Insecurities guide, though unseen.

Trading roles, can't you see?
You relishing my past's bittersweet spree
While I follow my routines, late to bloom,
Awaiting the reunion, distant as the moon.

Midsummer dreams, where do you roam,
Floating in the heated ocean's foam.
Free soul, unburdened by weight,
Before winter returns with its chilling fate.

I'll be your sunshine through the chill,
In winter's grasp, when weariness fills,
No more sickness, no more delay,
In my embrace, find peace and stay.

Endless work catches me each late night,
Days and nights blend in relentless flight.
My music playlist, dedicated to you,
Brews unspoken feelings overdue.

I want to mirror your mentality,
It fuels my focus and clarity.
By day's end, still feel the energy,
Enveloping me as I sleep peacefully.

When you return, your routine's relentless beat,
Aligns once more with my mindset, complete.
Then, you'll see how our reflections intertwine,
On the same path, our destinies align.

Number Letter Sequences

All these numbers, reminders of you and me,
Following our own patterns, our unique decree.
Each time they appear, I know we both ponder,
I wonder if it's the same for you yonder.

Letters of our names, a constant presence,
Follow me tirelessly in every instance.
Through daily tasks, they persistently flow,
Becoming tangible, in reality they grow.

In this silent state of stillness,
I grow stronger than ever, fearless.
No longer clinging to shadows past,
Ahead, bright visions align at last.

Amidst bustling surroundings, your socials
thrive,
Yet you seek solace in silent moments, alive.
Catching up with yourself in solitude's embrace,
Empathy blooms within, a gentle grace.

We've grown so much together,
Far apart, yet close within forever.
You know me, and I know you,
In dreams, we converse through codes true.
Chances are we've thought of each other,
Questioning our lives, pondering further.
Holding back, saving for a later day,
Knowing there'll be moments to find our way.

Nightly Reflections

Insecurity's grip, you might not see,
An instant cure, that's what it could be.
It's alright to seek attention, to feel,
Placing you high on a pedestal, real.

A subtle feeling, seeing through,
Seeking nods from admirers, few,
Or passing time, when boredom's due,
In search of something, maybe new.

New ideas or superficial tease,
Covering bruises, hoping for ease,
You can mend, on your own,
No need for those trivial tones.

Terrified of aging, inevitable someday,
Can't cling to this frivolous state, okay?
Since I got serious with you,
Caught you off guard, unsure what to do.

Deciding to release, at least for a while,
My heart's unspoken words, I can't compile.
No need for anyone to fathom this love,
Liberating my mind, surrendering thereof.

Tonight, thoughts of you, my prince, once more,
Longing to hold you close, to adore.
Silent thoughts of love, gentle and rare,
While I work hard each day, pursuing my
dreams with care.

Moon Glow

Beneath the midsummer moon's full glow,
What visions have we glimpsed, you know?
Let our souls entwine, let them flow,
Manifesting realness, watch it grow.

Far away, your habits hold you tight,
Walls seem unyielding, resisting the break.
Circles of people expand around,
Surface safety masking inner shadows.

Reveal your mystery, unseen,
Tonight, let it shine, serene.
Bathed in moonlight, beauty bright,
Your darkness now trades in the light.

Come closer to me, I care and adore you,
There is no rush for this sentimentality.
Don't give up on your strength,
I would be your faithful mentor.

No judgment here, only trust and grace,
Forgiveness blooms in this sacred space.
Rooted deep within, grounded and true,
Healing energies spread, embracing you.

Tonight you gaze at the full moon's gleam,
Sending secrets through the tranquil air.
Tonight I, too, behold the moon's beam,
Smiling as wishes drift with tender care.

Teddy Bear

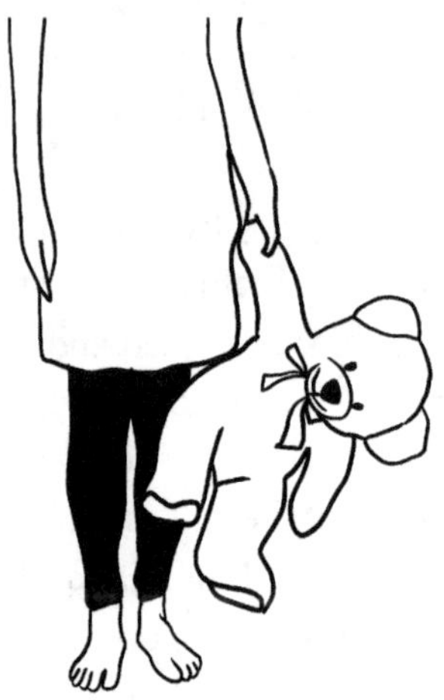

In this lifetime, souls search endlessly,
Beware the fear of endless seeking,
Too timid to firmly say yes,
As our souls linger in standby mode.

Embracing this familiar feeling,
Like an old friend, my teddy bear,
Warm, sweet, and comforting,
With you, it all feels true again.

I could mend my childhood fears,
No wonder I opened up to you.
You came back as my matching soul,
And so began this healing role.

You said no one has ever been so honest,
Awakening your deepest fears.
I became your loyal soul,
Always ready to catch you when you fall.

Suddenly, you fear it's too good to be true,
You've always worked so hard, it's what you do.
Your fears grow again, haunting your mind,
The past's trauma lingers, leaving scars behind.

I remain rooted as I've always been,
In your heart, you know where to return.
The teddy bear you cherished once,
All of me, you find your way back to.

Be in Silence

There must have been a delay,
Right at this moment in time.
We must have played it safe,
To shield ourselves right now.

We live in our heads these days,
So much to feel, in thought's maze.
Thinking it over, night after night,
Restless thoughts, rewinding in quiet.

No need for defeat, nor mind's game,
No control in this uncharted frame.
All we can do is come clean,
To our true selves, where reality gleams.

Realities laden with responsibilities,
You nodded, agreeing silently with ease.
I understand it all deeply, every part,
But why couldn't you speak your truth with me?

Sleepless nights, tasks to finish,
Your thoughts linger, refusing to diminish.
I prefer to stay in, find solace and mend,
In the purpose I've found, my efforts transcend.

In the quiet of our unspoken bond,
Do you doubt my need, misunderstood and
fond?
Subtle walls rise between us, unseen,
Yet I still rely on you, my constant unseen.

Hello

Guardian of the night,
Feel the change within,
Wanting to work it out,
Where have you been?

You wish you could come,
Take me away with you.
Our souls always connected,
Plotting our reunion now.

No one can hold a candle to you,
When good things happen, I want to write you.
You're my soulmate, sweet and true,
Plotting our journey, just us two.

Day to night, love stays true,
You're on my mind, each day anew.
Longing for our conversations, so fine,
Missing you dearly, your presence divine.

Once unkind, yet your heart beats for me,
Loved you then, love eternally.
Once cherished, forever will,
Always have, always will.

Telepathic messages, whispers in the night,
Your voice, a melody, pure and bright.
You're my greatest wish, shining through,
Always with you, forever true.

Songs play, remind me of you,
Melodies travel, air to you.
Fated connection, strong and true,
Do you still love me, too?

Every night, saying hello, our souls entwine,
Breaking through distance, time, and cosmic
design.
Your soul and mine, as one, align,
In this timeless dance, our hearts combine.

Healing

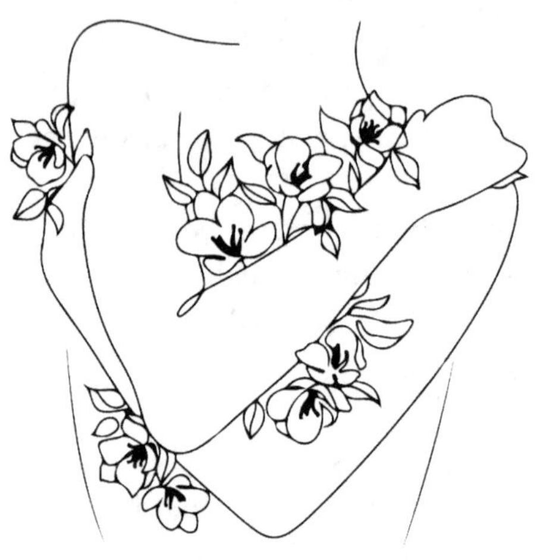

Every day, coincidences appear,
Around us, quietly and near.
Slowly showing, crystal clear,
One last pain, we must steer.

I shiver each time it comes near,
Craving solitude to reappear.
Nurturing my own sorrow,
Singing lullabies for tomorrow.

You feel the waves of feelings each time,
Trying to shut down your emotions' climb.
Tending to your own pain,
Finding balance in solitude's domain.

Tonight, we catch up to heal,
Lying on our own beds so still.
Gazing up at the ceiling above,
Wondering what's next with love.

We must let each other go,
For now, to heal and grow.
Reminders of you everywhere,
Gathering courage for our future to share.

Praying

This has come so close now,
On the edge of all emotions I've known.
More likely the stress I've been through,
A lot endured, yet untold to you.

Telling myself to stay strong, without fear,
If something triggers you today, my dear,
It's my attempt to connect, telepathy's grace,
Praying earnestly for everything to find its place.

I feel the past has slipped away,
Traumas, sadness, can't touch today.
Just need to pass this final test,
Will you follow me into what's next?

Take all the time you need with your past,
I understand how the journey can last.
Yet, I wonder what lies ahead,
Things won't be daunting, trust what I've said.

First, let's fulfill our current purposes,
Before our paths reunite, destiny assures.
Though the road ahead may stretch long,
They'll lead us back together where we belong.

Amidst swirling currents all around,
My heart's faith stays firm, profound.
With steadfast belief deep inside,
You are my destined realm, where destinies
coincide.

The Light in Your Smile - My Reflection

Change in my mind, came slow to start,
Yours arrived first, played its part,
Your change happened earlier, before mine,
I noticed lately, the shift in time.

In my healing, light has come,
Clear as your winter smiles spun,
Through the changes, time has shown,
Light like yours, I now own.

Needing this for evolution,
I accept more light within my soul,
Balanced by the moon's revolution,
Forgiveness and love, my higher goal.

Putting these puzzles all in line,
Now it makes sense, the grand design.
This mirrored bond we deeply hold,
In a blossoming garden of wisdom, pure and
bold.

The wheel of fortune spins in time,
Seeking solace in solitude we find.
Long have we tread this familiar path,
Reflecting on our journeys, alone yet aligned.

Under the moon's guiding light we roam,
Exploring mysteries along our shared journey,
What lies ahead remains unknown,
Yet my heart embraces our evolving
perspectives.

Labyrinth of Memories

Damage done, challenges arise,
Through day and night, I strive to rise.
Tasks await, much to achieve,
Before the new chapter I believe.

I know one thing for sure,
Opening up feels harder than before.
Yet love persists, steadfast and true,
Always returning, my heart beats for you.

Though I've built walls for everyone now,
Even for you, they stand tall somehow.
Alone seems safer, a choice I make,
Yet my heart longs for you, with every ache.

Reminiscing once more,
Life seemed simpler before.
Though distant, your smile still shines,
Freshening my memories like fine wines.

After these poems are done,
I may release a part of heaviness inside my
heart.
Only a fraction,
For I know it will forever remain with me.
Part of you will seek out mine,
Across worlds, distant and divine.
So much more our hearts will say,
In your cherished eyes, I'll forever stay.

Everlasting Union

I won't let this world crumble away,
Justice returns to light my way.
In this physical realm, no status, no flashy allure,
Only peace and helping hands endure.

The sun shines bright once more,
New ideas to explore.
I embrace my freedom deep within,
Welcome authenticity, where intentions begin.

You, out in the world, nightlife's allure,
Your stillness awakens thoughts pure.
When quiet settles, your mind wanders free,
Thoughts of you stir, connecting with me.

What I implemented in the connection,
You may want to be transparent.
Amidst the echo of external sway,
Intentions morph in the light of day.

It's alright to feel lost and overwhelmed,
Life's pressures weigh heavy, no need to pretend.
Yet within us, a flickering spark,
Of growing old together, lighting the dark.

The shift in foundational view will come in time,
Solidify intentional stability, a path to climb.
Follow your intuition, embrace spirituality's
flow,
Continuity, divine connection, as we grow.

Entwined in Unity

You and I, frozen in a glass conservatory,
Surrounded by fleshly flowers and crimson
butterflies,
Performing a silent ballet, a living artistry,
Where every move tells tales of love and
mysteries.

This leap of faith I choose to make,
Silently, towards what's at stake.
Though other duties call my name,
My heart's devotion to you remains the same.

This compassion I hold for you remains strong,
I wish you happiness, though you're not where
you belong.
My love for you, unwavering, always near,
Unconditional, steadfast, through joy and tears.

The realization you've unearthed within,
No longer hiding emotions meant for us.
A mix of fantasy woven with reality,
I embrace it all with you, eternally.

The rebirth of our bond,
Eagerly awaiting its renewal, so fond.
This time assured, we've grown mature,
Safeguarding each other's hearts, forever secure.

You and I, amidst the world's embrace,
Surrounded by nature's beauty and grace,
We align our shared dreams, now clear and true,
Each step forward, together, our dreams ensue.

www.ingramcontent.com/pod-product-compliance
Lightning Source LLC
La Vergne TN
LVHW050944200726
843508LV00011B/2437